Houseplants

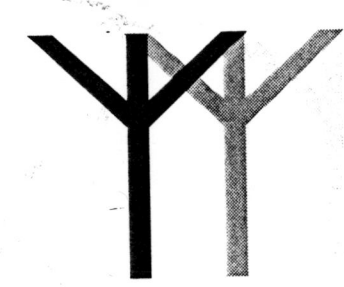

Cover: the Cape primroses, *Streptocarpus* hybrids, are among the most beautiful and reliable flowering houseplants

Overleaf: the many forms of *Coleus blumei*, the flame nettle, display a range of brilliant leaf colours (both photographs by Michael Warren)

Houseplants

A Wisley handbook
Ann Bonar

Cassell

The Royal Horticultural Society

Cassell Educational Limited
Artillery House
Artillery Row
London SW1P 1RT
for the Royal Horticultural Society

First published 1987

Bonar, Ann
  Houseplants.—New ed.—(A Wisley handbook).
  1. Houseplants
  I. Title   II. Royal Horticultural Society
  III. Series
  635.9′65   SB419

  ISBN 0-304-31146-4

Photographs by Michael Warren and Harry Smith
Collection
Design by Lesley Stewart

Phototypesetting by Chapterhouse, The Cloisters, Formby,
L37 3PX
Printed in Hong Kong by Wing King Tong Co. Ltd

Contents

Introduction

Growing houseplants is an absorbing hobby which can be expanded or contracted as you wish and which can take an enormous variety of forms. The range of plants available now is wider than it has ever been and in the modern home, with smoke-less fuel and natural gas, the selection is no longer limited by atmospheric pollution, as it was for the Victorians.

Many of today's plants are easily grown and do not necessarily want high temperatures, though these are much more common with central heating. But what they do need, with very few exceptions, is humidity. A moist atmosphere is as important as water and light, and its lack is one of the major causes of trouble with houseplants. Unfortunately, perhaps because it is invisible, it gets forgotten.

Once you start to grow plants indoors, you will find that you learn a good deal more about their requirements at such close quarters than when cultivating plants in the open. You are more likely to notice insects and diseases and will soon be able to differentiate between a healthy and a sick plant. With experience, a passing glance will remind you that a plant needs watering, whereas to the uninitiated it might appear quite normal.

Whether you are fascinated by large plants towering up to the ceiling, miniature African violets, plants with beautiful leaves or everlasting flowers, bromeliads or ferns, every room in the house can provide a home for some sort of plant and will be enhanced by it. Indeed, a home without plants looks bleak and unfurnished. Houseplants also offer a welcome outlet for frustrated gardeners living in flats.

Opposite: African violets, derived from *Saintpaulia ionantha*, are now available in various flower colours and forms as well as the original violet blue (see p.53)

Choosing plants to suit the home

Faced with a large selection of houseplants in a garden centre or shop, it is tempting to buy the one with the prettiest leaves or brightest flowers, take it home and expect it to live happily ever after. But it is much better to consider the conditions in your house first and then choose a plant which matches them in its cultivation needs.

For instance, you may feel that an ideal place for a houseplant is a corner on the landing, which is probably warm in winter but not very well lit at any time. A plant which does not mind shade or a temperature above 60°F (16°C) and is not too fussy about humidity would be suitable, such as mother-in-law's tongue (*Sansevieria trifasciata* 'Laurentii'), sweetheart vine (*Philodendron scandens*) or aspidistra. However, in poor light any flowering plant would gradually fade, become pale and elongated and fall victim to pests and diseases. Similarly, a brightly coloured foliage plant, such as dracaena or codiaeum, would also lose its colour and probably leaves as well.

By growing the right plant in the right place, you will be half way to successful cultivation. The same applies, of course, if you are given a plant as a present.

TYPES OF HOUSEPLANTS

Until the recent development of numerous flowering plants for the home, the typical houseplant was thought of as a pot plant with ornamental leaves. The variation of leaf shapes among foliage plants is enormous, when you consider the palms, the Swiss cheese plant (*Monstera deliciosa*), ivies, stag's-horn ferns, the umbrella tree (*Schefflera actinophylla*), vines and bromeliads. Add to that a rainbow of colours, from the yellow striping of the spider plant and *Dracaena fragrans* 'Massangeana' to the brilliance of the codiaeums, and who needs flowers? You can have just as striking a display with leafy plants as with flowers and one which lasts all the year round.

Foliage plants, if properly cared for, should reward their owners for several years. Flowering plants, on the other hand, are not quite so easy to grow successfully. Some have a much shorter life, sometimes only a few weeks, and are not intended to be grown for longer. Cinerarias and chrysanthemums, for example,

The large, curiously slashed leaves of the Swiss cheese plant, *Monstera deliciosa* (see p.49)

which bloom continuously and have often been specially treated to enable them to do so, must be regarded as 'throwaway' plants. Even so, they last a great deal longer than a bunch of cut flowers and in that sense give better value for money. Other plants, like the achimenes, the Cape primroses and the ever popular African violets, are especially useful as being both perennial and having a long flowering season.

The size of a plant is an important factor in making your selection – not only its size when you acquire it, but its potential size, together with its rate of growth. It is worth investigating how big a plant will eventually grow, before you buy it, and how fast, remembering that this will determine how often it needs repotting.

ARRANGEMENT AND DISPLAY

The possibilities for showing off houseplants and using them to decorate a home are endless. A windowsill is one of the most obvious places to put them, but be careful if it is south-facing, which can be too hot for many plants. There are numerous special

Tower pots and an attractive copper container hold a mixture of foliage plants

plant stands, including Victorian what-nots, wrought-iron containers on legs and vertical stands with ring attachments for pots, and all kinds of flat surfaces are suitable from tables to bookcases. Open shelving units are an excellent means of displaying plants, especially climbers and trailers, and can act as room dividers.

Hanging baskets, macramé hangers and pot hangers provide a cascade of greenery at different levels without taking up precious space on the floor or on furniture. A well-planted basket looks particularly good near a window and, with the new basket liners and attached saucers, there is no worry about drips after watering.

Climbing plants have great potential and, since many of them tolerate shade, can often be grown in areas of poor light away from windows. They require support and can be trained in various shapes or to go round doorways.

Houseplants grown in groups not only make more of an impact visually, but benefit one another too, because they give off water vapour from the leaves and create a locally humid atmosphere. You should choose plants with similar cultivation requirements for the purpose.

CONTAINERS

Containers are an integral part of any display and, like the plants, are available in a huge variety of designs, shapes and colours. The old heavy clay pots have largely given way to plastic pots, often with their own matching drip saucers, and as well as conventional pot shapes, there are squares, cylinders, troughs, urns and hanging baskets. A plain container may be concealed in a larger one of ceramic, plastic or another material, which does not have drainage holes and therefore protects the surface on which it is stood from drips. But be careful that the inner pot is not left permanently in water as a result. Sometimes, too, these outer containers are not fully waterproof and moisture may gradually seep through the base.

BUYING AND BRINGING HOME

Houseplants may be obtained from garden centres, florists' shops and chain stores, as well as from specialist nurseries (see p.64). On the whole, the standard is high and you should be able to start with a plant which is in good health, not starved, and free from pest or disease.

Look for plants whose foliage is a good dark green (those with leaves naturally variegated yellow or white generally have the word 'Variegata' or 'Aureomarginata' incorporated in their name, or sometimes 'Maculata' which means spotted). Avoid plants with leaves that are torn or decaying or have brown spots on them, with flowers that are wilting or faded, and with stems that are broken or mottled. Inspect them for pests such as greenfly on the backs of the leaves or clustered round the tips of shoots or even on the flower petals, and watch out particularly for red spider mite and scale insect, as they are very difficult to eradicate (see pp.34 and 35). Dry compost or roots protruding through the drainage holes may indicate that the plant has become weak through neglect and it is wiser not to buy it.

Fruiting in the winter months, the ornamental capsicum needs a sunny position (see p.40)

Houseplants may also be purchased at market stalls run by the Women's Institute or Townswomen's Guild; general street markets; village jumble sales and fetes; sales held by horticultural clubs and gardening societies; and plant fairs run by various charities, including the National Council for the Conservation of Plants and Gardens. Such outlets are often the source of rare or unusual plants unobtainable from normal commercial suppliers, but the quality is not always so reliable. There is also a risk that the plants may have been left outside too long before being sold.

When bringing a plant home, protect it from draughts and wind, preferably with a polythene bag or sheet, so that it does not lose moisture or become cold. Then keep it in a warm shaded place isolated from other plants for a few days, to prevent possible transmission of pests and diseases. Water well if necessary, repot into fresh compost if it appears cramped for root room, and maintain plenty of humidity (see pp.21 and 14). When it has settled down and all seems well, move it to its permanent position.

General care

LIGHT

In the open, plants receive light from all sides during the day, though sometimes it is rather dim, and have unlimited space for their roots to develop and so to absorb water and nutrients. Temperature and the humidity of the atmosphere vary, as does rainfall, and many plants have adapted themselves accordingly.

In a house, by contrast, the environment is almost completely artificial and a plant is wholly dependent on you for its healthy development. There is much less light available and therefore most plants need to be near a window or on a windowsill, though not necessarily in direct sunlight, to receive the maximum amount. However, a south-facing window will be too hot and bright in the summer and may even scorch the leaves. It is only suitable for cacti, pelargoniums and similar plants which are used to these conditions in their native habitats. Flowering plants and plants with variegated or coloured foliage usually require plenty of light, while plants with dark green foliage are often tolerant of shade and can be placed further from a window, perhaps three or four paces away. Do not move or turn a flowering plant which is covered in buds or these may drop off.

If a plant appears to be suffering from too much or too little light, the answer is simply to find a more suitable position for it. Be careful when watering not to leave large drops on the leaves, as these may cause scorch if hot sun shines through them. Plants can also be damaged if they are grown too close to glass, which sometimes magnifies the rays of the sun.

TEMPERATURE

A winter temperature above 60°F (16°C), which is the average in most homes, will suit the majority of houseplants and many do not thrive below 50°F (10°C). However, some definitely prefer to be cooler when flowering – cyclamen and azaleas, for instance, which are happier at about 55°F (13°C). A few are almost or completely hardy, notably tolmiea, aspidistra and ivy, and will not do well in higher temperatures. These are good for cool situations such as halls, landings and glass porches. In general the best temperature range for houseplants is between 50° and 80°F

The high humidity of a bathroom suits plants like ferns, asparagus and
Ficus benjamina

(10°–27°C), with 60° to 75°F (16–21°C) the optimum. A constant
temperature, without extreme changes between night and day,
and a position free from draughts, should be the aim for all plants.
Troubles such as falling or discoloured leaves or dropping buds
are easily prevented if these conditions are maintained.

HUMIDITY

Bound up with temperature, and just as important, is humidity.
The hotter the atmosphere, the more quickly does the water
vapour from the leaves evaporate, and the faster the roots must
absorb water from the compost. Much more stress is placed on
the plant and, if the atmosphere is dry as well as hot, water is lost
even more rapidly.

But a moist atmosphere results in a kind of pillow of water

vapour floating just above each leaf and slowing down the activity of the plant. Many houseplants are inhabitants of rain forests and, while it is obviously not possible or desirable to have the equivalent of a tropical downpour at intervals in the living room, humidity can be improved in various ways. Regular overhead misting or spraying with tepid water, ideally several times a day, will benefit most plants, except those with woolly or hairy leaves. Other methods are to place trays of water close to the plants, stand the pots on gravel in saucers of water, or simply grow them in groups (see p.11). It is particularly important to ensure a moist atmosphere in a centrally heated home, especially if the windows are double-glazed, and here a humidifier might be helpful.

Excess humidity is rarely a problem in the home. However, when plants show poor growth, lose their buds or flowers or develop brown leaves, the reason is often that the atmosphere is too dry and the humidity should therefore be increased.

WATERING

When a humid temperature is properly maintained, the need for watering is less. Humidity is just one of many variables determining how much and how often to give water, quite apart from the individual requirements of the plant concerned. These factors include the size of the pot, the material from which it is made, the type of compost, the rate of growth of the plant and its size, the temperature, the amount of light, and whether the plant is flowering, resting or simply growing.

As a general guide, water when the surface of the compost looks dry, or – another indication of dryness – when the container feels light in weight, especially if filled with peat-based compost. Give enough water to fill the space between the top of the compost and the rim of the pot and pour it on fairly rapidly. Then let it soak through and repeat, allowing the surplus to drain through; empty the saucer under the pot if necessary after about fifteen minutes.

Make sure that the compost never dries out completely during the growing season but, at the same time, do not let it remain wet for long periods. If you are in doubt about when to water, use a moisture meter. This is easy to read, efficient and inexpensive, and can be obtained from garden centres and sundriesmen.

Be careful to water peat-based composts thoroughly, otherwise the centre of the root ball of the plant may dry up completely. One sign that this has happened is when the plant requires much more frequent watering than usual, say every two instead of every five days. It is then difficult to wet right through again, except by immersing the root ball in water and leaving it there until sodden.

Cyclamen require careful watering, with the compost kept just moist (see p.42)

The same treatment is necessary when the compost has dried up so much as to shrink away from the sides of the container, with the result that water goes straight through the drainage holes without being absorbed.

Always use soft water, either rainwater or boiled water, or water which has been standing a day or two, both for watering and spraying. It should be at room temperature to avoid any shock to the roots. Do not get drops of water on the leaves, particularly hairy ones.

Both under- and over-watering can lead to various disorders and sometimes to the death of plants. Too dry a compost can usually be corrected by more frequent watering or soaking, without undue harm to the plant. However, a compost which is sodden and waterlogged can injure or kill the roots and in severe cases, even if the compost is allowed to dry out, it may be too late to save the plant.

If the compost seems very soggy, heavy or poorly structured and the plant looks unhappy, take it out of the container for a day.

Examine the root ball and remove any roots which are brown or dead, leaving only healthy white ones. Then, depending on the extent of the damage, either return to the original pot and withhold water until the surface of the compost has dried out; or repot in fresh compost, with drainage material at the bottom.

Plants with coloured foliage tend to produce more intense colours if kept slightly dry.

FEEDING

With watering goes feeding. Plants manufacture starches and oxygen in the presence of light through the green tissues of the leaves and stems. But they also need mineral nutrients in the growing medium, in the form of potassium, phosphorus and magnesium and many other elements, which the roots absorb at the same time as moisture.

Modern composts are carefully formulated to provide a balanced blend of both bulky constituents, such as peat or loam, and minerals. These nutrients last for varying lengths of time and only after the plant has used them all up will supplementary feeding with a compound fertilizer be necessary. There are numerous brands available, which have been specially prepared for houseplants to give the correct balance of nutrients. Foliage plants benefit from a high proportion of nitrogen, which promotes leaf and stem growth, and flowering plants from potassium and phosphorus, which are important for flowering. Labels show the percentage of nutrients present in the compound, indicated by the symbol N (nitrogen), K (potassium) and P (phosphorus).

Dry fertilizer may be applied in the form of pellets, tablets or sticks, which are pushed into the compost, or as a powder sprinkled on the surface (be careful not to get it on the leaves). These dissolve when the plant is watered, releasing the fertilizer slowly over a period of several weeks, and usually need to be added only once or twice during the growing season. Liquid feeding, on the other hand, consists of dissolving a small quantity of concentrated fertilizer or fertilizer solution in water, at the dilution rate specified by the manufacturer, and then watering it into the compost. Depending on the maker's instructions, liquid fertilizer is generally given about once a week or fortnight, when the plants are in full growth, which in most cases means April to October. No feeding is required when plants are resting and not actively growing, which normally occurs in winter. Some plants such as cyclamen and azaleas should only be fed after they have finished flowering.

17

Plants which have become undernourished and lacking in all food materials through neglect will generally recover if they are repotted in fresh compost. This should supply the necessary nutrients. Plants can also be affected by overfeeding, so don't be tempted to use fertilizers as a universal cure.

A shortage or excess of a specific nutrient, such as potassium or nitrogen, may be remedied by increasing or decreasing the amount of the mineral concerned. The condition known as chlorosis often develops on plants growing in alkaline compost, which have been watered with hard tap water. It indicates iron or manganese deficiency and is best dealt with by repotting in acid compost and using soft water.

GROOMING AND TRAINING

Some discreet attention to detail can make your plants look as perfect as other people's. Dead flowers, damaged or yellowing leaves and broken stems should be removed before they rot or fall. Foliage plants in particular should have the leaves washed or sponged regularly to remove dust and spray marks and keep them glossy. Proprietary leaf-cleaning agents may also be used, following the manufacturer's instructions, and some of them incorporate an insecticide as well.

Climbing plants will need to be trained up a support, such as canes, split canes, a plastic frame, a miniature trellis or wires. If they have aerial roots, a moss stick is ideal. This is a pole surrounded with damp sphagnum moss or fibrous peat and bound with wire, or a tube of plastic netting filled with moss or peat. Tie in the stems of climbers as they grow with fillis (soft string) or plastic-covered wire ties, and break off the tips just above a leaf or pair of leaves when they have grown tall enough. Trailing plants can be left to their own devices, but checking their growth in the same way will make them leafier and encourage flowering.

Some plants like *Monstera deliciosa* and *Ficus elastica* 'Decora' can grow so large that they reach the ceiling and become difficult to accommodate. The top of the main stem may be cut back to a convenient height and the sideshoots too may be trimmed, each time making the cut just above a leaf or pair of leaves. (The severed bits can sometimes be used as cuttings; see p.28).

Opposite, above: azaleas should not be fed until they have finished flowering (see p.51)

Below: the devil's ivy, *Epipremnum aureum* (*Scindapsus aureus*), may be trained to a support or allowed to trail (see p.44)

Alternatively, the size can be controlled in advance by reducing the root ball when repotting in spring. Use a knife to cut round the sides and base of the root ball and slice away about a quarter, which will provide room for fresh compost when the plant is returned to a container of the same size. The plant will be stimulated by injury to produce new roots and will have a new supply of food with which to carry on this process.

On variegated plants, any plain green shoot or stem which appears should be cut back to the point of origin to preserve the variegation.

TOOLS

The main tool for working with houseplants is a pair of hands. Other useful implements are an old dinner fork, for breaking up a hard smooth compost surface; small and large watering cans; a mister or sprayer and a separate one for pesticides – a pint (half litre) size is convenient; soft string or ties; scissors or secateurs; and either a marked measure or a set of measuring spoons for fertilizers and pesticides. Meters are useful though not essential, for determining water or nutrient content of the compost, available light, humidity and temperature, but they should not be relied on for absolute accuracy. A soil-testing kit, which shows whether the compost is acid, neutral or alkaline, might be helpful, particularly for lime-hating plants such as azaleas.

COMPOSTS

Composts for plants in containers are of two types – soil-based and peat-based or soilless. The soil-based ones consist of a mixture of good soil, i.e. loam, peat and sand, together with nutrients and chalk. The John Innes range of potting composts, which is probably the best known, is made up to a specific formula and comes in three grades numbered 1, 2 and 3, the last two containing respectively twice and three times as much nutrient and chalk as the first. JI No 1 is suitable for small plants in containers of up to 4 inches (10 cm) diameter and also for rooting cuttings; No 2 is for pots of between 4 and 7 inches (10–17.5 cm) and is perhaps the best all-purpose compost; and No 3 is for large plants growing in containers of 7 inches (17.5 cm) or more. A soil-based compost is particularly recommended for vigorous strong-rooting plants in permanent containers.

The peat-based composts consist largely of peat, with fine sand but no loam, plus varying amounts of nutrients and chalk depending on the manufacturer. These are conveniently packaged, light to carry and easy to handle. Many of them now incorporate a wetting agent, which makes them easier to wet if they dry out. A peat-based compost is usually preferable for bromeliads and other tree-dwelling plants.

Specially prepared composts, often known as ericaceous, are available for acid-loving plants like azaleas and adiantums, and there are also composts with extra grit designed for cacti.

POTTING AND REPOTTING

If a plant grows rapidly and the root tips start to emerge from the drainage holes, it should be given a larger container and fresh compost, otherwise it will become stunted and may die. However, some plants flower better if slightly pot-bound and some large permanent plants have to be kept in the same size of container for reasons of space.

To repot, take a pot about 2 inches (5 cm) larger than the previous one, and if it is a clay pot, put a few crocks in the bottom to stop the drainage hole becoming blocked. Then fill the base with a little compost. Knock the old container against the edge of the work surface to loosen the plant, tip it out gently and sit it on top of the new compost. If any long roots have become wound round and round the outside, cut these back to the surface of the root ball, but otherwise do not disturb the plant. Pack compost in down the sides of the pot, firming it round the root ball, until it is level with the top of the root ball. This should leave a space for watering of about $\frac{1}{2}$ to 2 inches (1.5–5 cm) below the rim of the container, depending on its size. Water well to soak and settle the compost.

Many permanent plants need repotting each year in spring, just as growth is starting again. Bulbs for Christmas should be potted in early autumn and cacti can be done in early to late summer.

A less laborious alternative to annual repotting is top dressing. A 2-inch (5 cm) layer of the old compost is removed, disturbing the roots as little as possible, and replaced with fresh compost. However, the plant will then require much more feeding than in the previous growing season.

WINTER TREATMENT

Most houseplants rest naturally in winter, from October to March in the northern hemisphere, when light is greatly decreased both in duration and intensity. At the same time, growth is slowed down by lower temperatures and the need for water is thus much reduced. You should in general give enough water to keep the

Above: plenty of water is necessary for the winter-flowering poinsettia, *Euphorbia pulcherrima* (see p. 44)

Below: the aluminium plant, *Pilea cadieri*, needs a minimum temperature of 50°F (10°C) in winter (see p.51)

compost just moist, only increasing the amount if a plant shows signs of growing. In other words, continue to adjust the quantity of water as you do in summer, but be prepared to water much less and at longer intervals. Too much water in winter is one of the major causes of death in houseplants.

Regular watering will of course be necessary for the minority of plants which grow in winter, especially flowering plants such as cyclamen.

Too high a temperature during winter can also lead to trouble, as it may force the plant into growth which is weak owing to poor light. This is often when pest infestation becomes rampant. A day-time temperature about 10°F (5°C) above the minimum required for the plant concerned is the most suitable.

HOLIDAYS

Some thought must be given to the care of houseplants when you are away for more than two or three days and can't ask a neighbour or friend to look after them.

In the summer put the plants in a cool but well-lit part of the house and water them thoroughly, or place them in a bath with about $\frac{1}{2}$ inch (1.5 cm) of water in it. Another method is to group them together beneath a large bowl of water and to run lengths of water-absorbent material from this to the compost in each pot. Thick cotton thread, flannel, towelling or capillary matting may be used and will act as a wick supplying water from the reservoir. The plants may be covered with a tent of clear polythene sheeting to keep the air moist and decrease the rate of water absorption, though this will cut down their light. Remove any decaying vegetation first, otherwise it will rapidly infect healthy tissue in the enclosed humid conditions.

An easier solution to the problem is to use self-watering containers. These have a water reservoir in the base and wicks which automatically regulate the supply of water. Or you can reduce the need for watering in advance, by incorporating the special water-absorbent granules now available into the compost when potting.

In winter, the difficulty lies not so much in watering as in the temperature. If the house is not heated, the temperature can easily fall to 40°F (4°C), which is too low for plants of tropical origin. However, if heating can be provided, the temperature should be low enough to reduce the need for watering, but high enough to ensure survival of the plants.

Specialist care*

CACTI

Cacti make fine houseplants: they do not need a great deal of attention, some have beautiful flowers and they stand up well to central heating. They will also tolerate neglect better than most indoor plants.

They require very good drainage and are best grown in specially prepared compost containing plenty of grit. Generally speaking, except for the Christmas cactus, water in spring, summer and autumn as you would an ordinary houseplant, but in winter keep the compost almost completely dry, watering about once a month. Cacti need all the light you can provide throughout the year and high temperatures in summer, although in winter many of them should be kept at a temperature of about 45°F (7°C). On the whole, the lower the temperature, the drier the compost should be.

Repot mature cacti every two or three years, either in spring or in summer after flowering and feed after flowering in the second and third year. They flower better if slightly short of root room. (See also the Wisley handbook on cacti.)

BROMELIADS

Bromeliads are a family of plants mostly native to the tropical forests of South America, where they grow high up in the branches and forks of trees, or sometimes on the ground among rocks. They do not absorb food and water from the trees, but simply use them as supports and take in nourishment from the atmosphere and from rotting vegetation. As a result the root system is small.

Most bromeliads consist of a rosette of leaves, flat and star-like or more upright, forming a central funnel in which rainwater collects and from the centre of which come the flowers. The leaves are attractively marked and coloured and the flowers may be brilliant and long-lasting.

They need shallow containers filled with a peat-based compost, or can be made into a bromeliad 'tree'. This is done by binding

*Orchids are not included in this book; see the Wisley handbook on the subject.

The distinctive, brighly coloured rosettes of the bromeliad *Neoregelia carolinae* 'Tricolor'

fibrous peat to forks in a dead branch, on which the plants are placed and secured with twine or plastic-covered wire until they have anchored themselves with the root.

Water is poured into the funnel, which should be kept full in summer and nearly empty in winter, and the compost must be barely moist at all times. Some, like *Aechmea fasciata*, will grow in average humidity, others such as guzmanias require a very moist atmosphere. Feeding is not very important and the plants are happy in good light or a little shade. The temperature should mostly be moderate, 60 to 65°F (16–18°C), but higher while the offsets are forming, at 70°F (21°C) or more. After flowering, the parent plant eventually dies and is replaced by offsets.

BULBS

Spring bulbs can be grown in bulb fibre or, if you want them to flower every year, in standard potting compost. In this case, you will have to feed them with a proprietary fertilizer when flowering has finished and let the leaves turn yellow and die down naturally, in order to supply food to develop the embryo flower. A resting period should follow, usually in July and August,

A conservatory is a good place for a rampant climber like the passion flower, *Passiflora caerulea* (left), and also for plants such as the winter cherry, *Solanum capsicastrum* (right), which benefit from plenty of light (see pp.49 and 55)

when little or no water is given, after which they can be repotted in fresh compost.

Bulbs which have been prepared for forcing are potted and watered in late August or early September, then put in a dark cool place for about three months to form roots. Once the shoots have emerged, they may be brought indoors to flower within a few weeks. Ordinary compost or bulb fibre can be used, or the bulbs may be grown in bulb glasses with the roots in water. If you want them to flower again after growing in bulb fibre or water, they should be well fed until the leaves die down and planted outside in spring. They are no good for further forcing indoors.

BOTTLE GARDENS

A large clean carboy of green or clear glass is the best container for a bottle garden, but any large bottle or old sweet jar may be used. A tight-fitting bung or stopper, preferably of cork, is essential to prevent evaporation. About five or six plants should be sufficient and planting is easier if you sketch out the arrangement on a sheet of paper first. Small leafy slow-growing plants are recommended. *Pilea cadierei*, maidenhair ferns, small-leaved ivies, *Pteris cretica* 'Albo-Lineata', mosaic plants, *Peperomia caperata*, cryptanthus and small creeping figs would all be good choices.

The growing medium is made up in layers, starting with drainage material such as shingle 1 to 2 inches (2.5–5 cm) deep, then charcoal $\frac{1}{4}$ inch (3 mm) deep, and finally potting compost at least 2 inches (5 cm) deep. Pour each ingredient in turn down a paper funnel into the base of the bottle, spread it out evenly and firm it down with a cotton reel attached to a cane. Make the planting holes and insert the plants with a pair of long-handled tongs or with old dinner forks attached to canes, firming them in with the cotton reel. At the end of planting, water with a long thin-spouted watering can or tube, directing the water down the sides of the container. Use just enough to moisten the compost, which will not be a great deal, then put in the bung. If the condensation inside doesn't disappear in a day or two, remove the bung temporarily. If there is no condensation at all, add a little more water. After that, the bottle garden will require virtually no attention, apart from spraying with water about every six months, and it should last several years before the plants become too large.

CONSERVATORIES

Those houseplant owners who are lucky enough to have a glass porch or conservatory can experiment with a much greater selection of plants. The extra light means that many more flowering plants may be grown successfully, including bougainvillea, gardenia, cytisus, plumbago and stephanotis, and bigger plants, for example, camellia, abutilon and hydrangea, can be allowed to develop fully. A conservatory in particular is a good place for houseplants in the summer and is useful for reviving any that are flagging in the enclosed conditions of the home and for bringing on young plants for indoor decoration.

Propagation

PLANTLETS AND OFFSETS

It is always fun to try to increase your own plants. Even if you have never done it before, there is one foolproof method – and that is using plantlets already produced by the parent. The spider plant (*Chlorophytum*) and mother-of-thousands (*Saxifraga stolonifera*) are two which form perfect tiny plants at the ends of long stems, complete with roots. If cut off and planted in 2-inch (5 cm) diameter pots of moist potting compost in spring or summer, they will start to grow at once.

Offsets are miniature plants growing from the base of the parent at soil level. They occur on the urn plant (*Aechmea fasciata*) and daffodils, among others. They can be removed and planted separately in summer or autumn.

DIVISION

Division is another easy method of propagation, used mostly for herbaceous, not woody, houseplants, for instance the Cape primrose (*Streptocarpus*), African violets (*Saintpaulia*) and mother-in-law's tongue (*Sansevieria*). When repotting, you will see that the crown of the plant naturally falls into three or four parts, each with a central rosette. These will form new plants if you cut carefully between them, making sure that each has some roots attached. They should be planted in individual pots at once and will quickly establish and may even flower the same year.

CUTTINGS

Cuttings can be taken from many plants, especially shrubs, trailers and climbers. It is easy to make the cutting itself, but the difficulty comes in supplying the right conditions to encourage it to root.

A cutting usually consists of a short length of stem taken from the top of a new non-flowering shoot less than a year old. A tip or soft stem cutting, the sort most often used, is 2 to 3 inches (5–7.5cm) long, generally needs warmth to root and does so quickly in two or three weeks. It is worth taking several cuttings at a time as a precaution and you can also dip the ends of the cuttings in hormone rooting powder. Soft cuttings are most likely

Busy lizzies, *Impatiens* cultivars, are easily increased from tip cuttings (see p.46)

to root from late May to early July, though geraniums are traditionally left until August.

To make a cutting, cut off the tip of the stem just below a leaf joint and remove the lower leaves or pairs of leaves, usually one or two. Make sure that the cut surface is clean, without ragged edges, and if necessary, recut or trim it up with a sharp knife or razor blade. Using a 3 to $3\frac{1}{2}$-inch (7.5–9 cm) pot, fill it with a light potting compost such as JI No 1 or a special cuttings compost, make a hole at the edge with a stick or dibber and insert the cutting to half its length. The cut end must rest securely on the compost and it should be firmed in well so that a gentle tug on a leaf does not loosen it. Put as many cuttings round the edge of the pot as can be fitted in without the leaves touching and water them in. Then place the pot in a propagator with base heating and trans-parent cover, or enclose it in a clear plastic bag, blown-up and

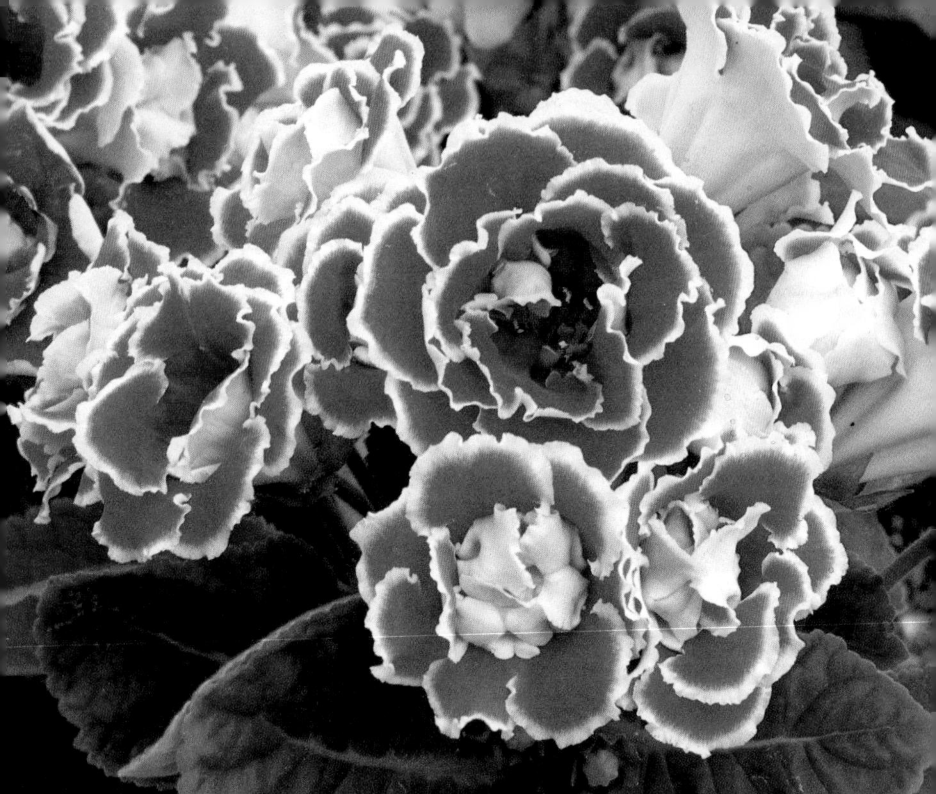

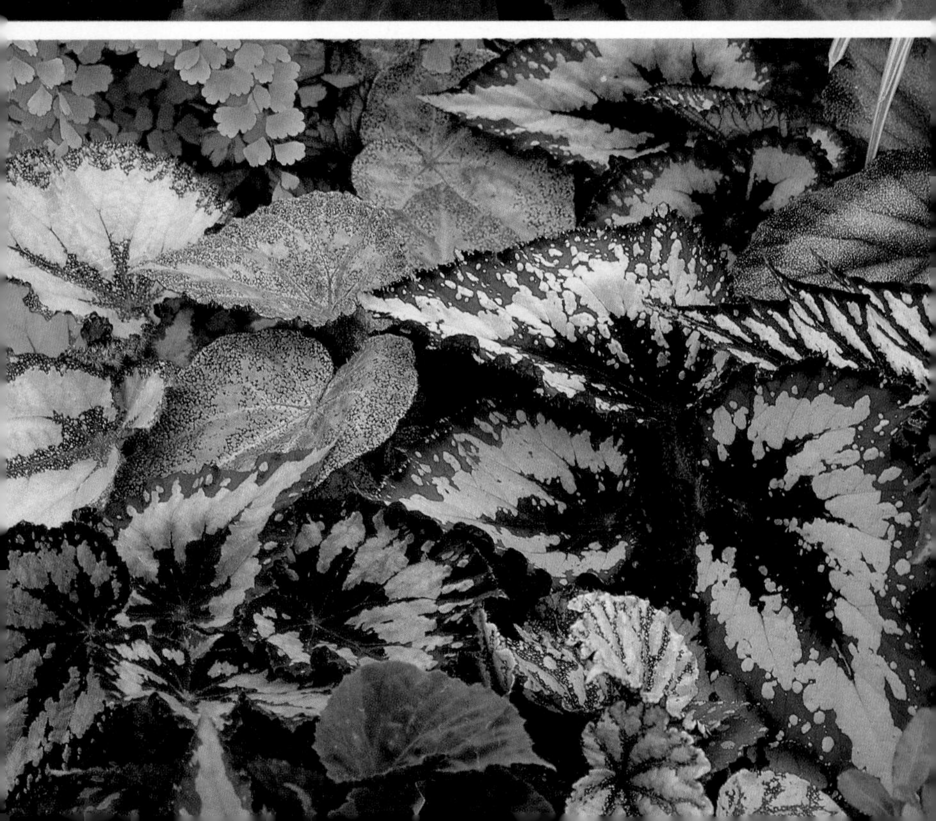

secured round the rim with an elastic band. Keep out of direct sunlight and maintain a humid atmosphere, by spraying if required, to prevent the leaves losing too much water and drying up before the stem has started to grow roots. All cuttings should be potted as soon as they have been made, except those of cacti which should be left for a few days to form a dry callus on the cut surface. After rooting, pot the cuttings separately in individual pots of a size to take the roots without cramping them.

A few houseplants, including African violets and rex begonias, can be increased by leaf cuttings. (Details of this method are given under the plant concerned in the alphabetical list, pp.36–58.)

SEED

A number of houseplants, such as busy lizzies and coleus, can be raised from seed and in recent years the range has expanded to include geraniums and African violets and some exotic new introductions. It is obviously a much less expensive method of obtaining a new houseplant than buying fully grown specimens, and you can be certain that it will be healthy and free from pests and diseases from the start of its life.

Work with a proprietary peat-based seed or light potting compost; the latter is quite suitable if you are short of time and wish to leave seedlings where they are until a few inches tall. Use small pots or plastic cartons with drainage holes in the base, fill them with compost, lightly firm down and level the surface, and water to moisten. Then sow the seeds thinly and evenly on the surface and cover them with a thin layer of finely sieved compost, firming it gently. Spray the surface with water and place the containers in a heated propagator or an airing cupboard. Temperatures vary in the range of 65 to 80°F (18–30°C), but most houseplants are tropical and need high temperatures. They should normally be kept dark, covered in black polythene, although some require light for germination. For individual plants, follow the instructions on the seed packet. Once germination has begun, bring the seedlings into the light and make sure that they never run short of water.

Opposite above: the spectacular gloxinias, Sinningia hybrids, may be raised from seed sown from October to March (see p.55)
Below: rex begonias can be propagated from leaf cuttings (see p.38)

Disorders, diseases and pests

Many of the common troubles of houseplants arise from unsuitable growing conditions, rather than from diseases and pests. The usual symptoms include discoloured foliage, poor growth and lack of flowers – often produced for totally different reasons. However, these disorders are easily remedied by meeting the correct requirements of light, temperature, humidity, watering and feeding, as described on pp.13–23.

Minor outbreaks of a pest or disease can often be controlled without resorting to chemicals. Indeed, pests like red spider mite become resistant to pesticides which are used regularly. However, if chemical controls are necessary, they should be used with caution, particularly when there are children or pets in the house.

Some houseplants may be damaged by chemical pesticides. Always follow the manufacturer's instructions. Do not spray in extreme temperatures, bright sunlight or when plants are dry at the roots and avoid spraying open blooms.

DISORDERS

Symptoms	Possible causes
Lower leaves turn yellow and fall	Sudden drop in temperature. Draughts.
Gradual yellowing of leaves, usually starting at bottom, eventually falling; whole plant may die	Overwatering, compost too wet.
Yellow blotches on leaves or leaves completely yellow before falling	Underwatering.
Upper leaves becoming rapidly yellow or bleached, mottled or speckled	Chlorosis – manganese or iron deficiency.
Leaves light green or yellow, sometimes orange or red; plant straggly and slow-growing	Shortage of nutrients, particularly nitrogen.
Leaves pale or bleached; plant thin, weak and drawn	Lack of light.
Variegated or coloured leaves lose markings or fade	Lack of light. Reversion. Compost too moist.
Yellow or white rings on leaves, especially achimenes, African violets, gloxinias	Roots chilled by cold water. Water splashes on leaves.

Symptoms	Possible causes
Brown spots on leaves	Overwatering. Overfeeding. Excess sun. Dry fertilizer on leaves. Too cold, for cacti.
Raised corky patches on undersurface of leaves, especially ivy-leaved pelargoniums, peperomias	Oedema or dropsy – from excessive humidity or overwatering (do not remove affected leaves).
Irregular rusty spots becoming sunken, on cacti	Corky scab – from exposure to sunlight, or lack of light and too much humidity.
Leaves brown, particularly at tips and margins	Insufficient humidity. Draughts. Compost too alkaline. Potassium deficiency. Too much sun for shade-loving plants.
Brown patches on leaves before falling	Underwatering.
Large pale brown patches, later papery, on leaves, especially African violets	Sun scald.
Red patches or streaks on leaves, also on stalks and bulbs, of hippeastrums	Inadequate watering.
Leaves fall without discolouring, or sometimes first turn purplish or silver	Draughts. Sudden drop in temperature. Cold water on roots.
Leaves limp, whole plant wilting	Compost dry or too wet.
Buds or flowers drop prematurely	Draughts. Disturbance to plant by moving or turning. Atmosphere dry. Lack of light. Chilling of roots with cold water. Too little water when buds developing, particularly azaleas. Excessive watering.
Failure to flower	Insufficient light and warmth in growing season. Lack of food. Potassium deficiency. Excess of nitrogen, particularly if abundant leafy growth. Plant pruned wrongly and flowering growth cut off. Temperature too high during storing or forcing bulbs. Compost dry when hyacinths kept in dark.
Failure to fruit	Atmosphere dry. Shortage of food, particularly potassium. Compost dry. Temperature too high.

DISEASES

Symptoms	Cause, treatment and prevention
White powdery spots on leaves and sometimes on stems and flowers, especially begonias, African violets	Powdery mildew. Remove badly affected leaves; spray with benomyl. Plants which are dry at roots are more susceptible, so keep compost moist.
Greyish brown fur on leaves and other parts; sometimes many small red or brown spots on petals, especially cyclamen	Grey mould. Remove dead and dying tissues promptly to prevent infection and spray with benomyl.
Black or brown rotting at base of stems; plant wilting or collapsing	Foot, crown and root rots. Water with cheshunt compound or dust base with bordeaux powder; in severe cases, remove all dead parts including roots and repot. Use sterilized compost and pots and clean water.
Orange powdery pustules on leaves, mainly undersurfaces, of fuchsias, cinerarias; masses of chocolate-coloured spores, on pelargoniums	Rusts. Remove and burn infected leaves; spray with carbendazim; in severe cases destroy plant. Avoid splashing leaves with water.
Thickened leaves and swollen buds turning grey, on azaleas	Azalea gall. Pick off and burn galls; spray with mancozeb.
Leaves mottled, blotched or striped with pale green, yellow or black, also distorted; plant stunted and flowers may be malformed or marked	Viruses, e.g. cucumber mosaic, tomato spotted wilt. Destroy any plant with these symptoms.

PESTS

Symptoms	Cause and treatment
Leaves sticky and covered with black sooty patches; tiny transparent spots on undersides; clouds of small white insects fly up when disturbed	Whitefly. When flies visible, spray undersides of leaves with permethrin; sponge leaves. Early treatment important.
Young leaves yellowing, curling or distorted; foliage sticky, soiled with sooty mould and white flakes; small black, pink, green or yellowish insects on shoot tips, buds and leaves	Aphids (greenfly). Spray with permethrin or pirimicarb; sponge leaves.
Yellowish speckling or greyish tinge on leaves, which may dry up; plant draped in webbing; minute yellowish green or reddish insects present	Red spider mite. Isolate plant; increase humidity and watering and reduce temperature. Spray thoroughly with malathion or dimethoate three times at weekly intervals. Resistant strains common. Most plants susceptible, particularly in summer.

Symptoms	Cause and treatment
Fluffy white blobs on leaves and at stem joints; leaves dull and plant tired-looking	Mealy bugs; and root mealybugs. Pick off; spray with malathion, or dab insects with methylated spirits.
Small flat or raised yellowish or dark brown spots on leaves and stems; sticky and sooty patches, especially calamondins, ficus	Scale insects. Spray with dimethoate three times at fortnightly intervals; sponge leaves.
Coarse pale mottling of leaves; small yellow and grey insects which hop off when disturbed; white specks on undersides of leaves	Leafhoppers. Spray with permethrin.
Tiny black and white or orange insects on leaves; foliage lightly flecked and silvered	Thrips. As for leafhoppers.
Flowers and young leaves distorted; no new growth on plant; microscopic mites on buds and shoot tips, especially cyclamen, begonias and African violets	Tarsonemid mites. Burn any affected plant.
Sinuous white or beige lines on leaves, especially chrysanthemums, cinerarias	Leafminers. Remove and burn affected leaves. Spray with HCH or pirimiphos-methyl at first sight.
Sudden collapse and death of plant; irregular notches in edges of leaves	Vine weevil – soil-dwelling maggots destroying roots and bulbs (adult beetles eat into leaves). Water with spray strength HCH or permethrin in late July and late August. Particularly active autumn to spring. Control difficult.
Small greyish black flies around plant or on surface of compost	Fungus gnats (sciarids), with thin white maggots feeding on decaying organic matter in soil. Remove dead leaves and mix diazinon granules into top of compost; control adults with houseplant aerosol. A nuisance but not harmful to established plants.
Tiny white insects hopping on surface of compost and burrowing back	Springtails. Often abundant in peat-based compost and brought out by watering. Entirely harmless.
Large holes in leaves	Slugs and snails. Caterpillars. Earwigs. Pick off by hand.

A selection of houseplants

The following list of houseplants is arranged alphabetically by genus, with asterisks to indicate ease of cultivation. Thus: * = easy to grow; ** = moderately easy; *** = temperamental. The abbreviation MWT denotes the minimum winter temperature required.

Botanical names are constantly changing, but as far as possible those which are now considered valid have been given, with cross references where necessary under the more familiar names.

Achimenes.* The hot-water plant is a delightful bushy, or sometimes trailing plant about 1 ft (30 cm) tall, with masses of open trumpet-shaped flowers from June to November. The most common colours are blue and purple, but pink, white, red and yellow are also available. It grows from small tubers, which should be planted 2 in. (5 cm) apart and ½ in. (1.5 cm) deep in early spring, in a temperature of 65°F (18°C). Keep well lit but out of direct sunlight and water thoroughly – with warm water is said to be best. Support the upright kinds and nip out the tips to keep them bushy. After flowering, dry off the tubers and store them over winter in frost-free conditions, MWT 50°F (10°C).

Adiantum. Some of the prettiest and most delicate ferns are the maidenhairs. A. capillus-veneris** has graceful black stems which grow to about 1 ft (30 cm) and then arch over, carrying thin, filmy, triangular leaves, toothed along one edge. It makes a good plant for macramé hangers in the bathroom, where it gets the very humid atmosphere essential to it. Another maidenhair, A. raddianum 'Fragrantissimum',** is slightly scented. They require a little shade, not too much warmth about 60–70°F (16–21°C) and moist acid compost. Draughts and a dry atmosphere result in browning and withering of the leaflets. Increase by division.

Aechmea. Sometimes called the urn plant, A. fasciata* is a bromeliad with strap-shaped leaves 1 ft (30 cm long), of grey-green banded with silver. They form a deeply centred rosette, the 'urn' or funnel for water, from the centre of which comes the bright pink flowerhead with small blue flowers in summer, lasting several months. It is easily grown in a peat-based compost; MWT 50°F (10°C). Increase by cutting off the offsets when about 6 in. (15 cm) tall and potting individually in 3-in. (7.5-cm) pots. Each plant flowers only once and then dies.

Other bromeliads needing similar conditions include Ananas (pineapple); Billbergia; Neoregelia; Vriesea; and Guzmania, although this requires very high humidity.

Agave. The century plant, A. americana,* can grow very large indeed, up to 25 ft (7.5 metres) tall in the open, but the form with yellow-edged leaves, 'Marginata', is much smaller and slow-growing. Quite distinct from this is the neat and small A. victoriae-reginae,* whose dark green leaves are tipped and edged with white, growing upright in a cluster to about 6 in. (15 cm). Agaves are succulents and store water in their leaves, so the compost can be allowed to dry between waterings for a day or two. In winter, however, water only about once a month and keep cool, MWT 45–50°F (7–10°C). Plenty of light, with sun and average temperatures in summer, are suitable and humidity is not important. Increase by sideshoots, if produced, or by seed.

Above: *Achimenes* (left), from tropical America, prefers warm water –
hence its common name; *Aphelandra squarrosa* (right) has beautifully
striped leaves, with yellow flowers as a bonus (see p.38)

Below: *Asparagus densiflorus* 'Sprengeri' (left) is ideal for a hanging
basket; the popular Reiger begonias (right) were developed quite
recently in Germany (see pp.38 and 39)

Aloe. The partridge-breasted aloe, *A. variegata*,* is an attractive succulent. Its upright leaves grow in a rosette and are triangular in cross-section, white-edged and with dark brown bands on a green background; height is about 6 in. (15 cm). *A. humilis** has similarly upright leaves, but in a much looser rosette and toothed and spiny. Both may be treated in the same way as agaves.

Ananas. See under *Aechmea*.

Aphelandra. The zebra plant, *A. squarrosa*,** is a bushy evergreen shrub in its native Brazil. The white-striped leaves need high humidity and it should be frequently watered to maintain the bright yellow flower spikes, appearing in December and January. Height is about 15 in. (38 cm). Draughts result in leaf drop and the temperature should be at least 65°F (18°C), with good light. If cut down after flowering to leave 3 in. (7.5 cm) of stem and rested for a few weeks, the plant will sprout new shoots and can be repotted and grown on (see p.37).

Araucaria. The Norfolk Island pine, *A. heterophylla* (*A. excelsa*),* comes from the Pacific island of that name and is related to the monkey puzzle tree. A graceful, evergreen, upright plant with frond-like shoots and leaves, it is easily grown to 3 ft (90 cm) or more and will tolerate a little shade; MWT 40°F (4°C). Repot in spring. Good humidity will prevent red spider mite, to which it is prone.

Asparagus. The asparagus ferns, *A. densiflorus* 'Sprengeri',* and *A. setaceus* (*A. plumosus*),* are very different in appearance: the first has long trailing stems with needle-like leaves all along their length, while the second has feathery triangular leaves and is much used by florists. Both are related to the edible vegetable. Good humidity will prevent leaf fall and some shade is necessary; MWT 40°F (4°C). Water normally. They can be divided for increase and any stems which become straggly cut back to soil level to encourage new growths (see p.37).

Aspidistra. Sometimes known as the cast iron plant, *A. elatior** was popular in Victorian times, often associated with antimacassars and chenille tablecloths. It stands up well to neglect and pollution and will grow in shade. Its handsome evergreen leaves, glossy and gracefully arching, can grow to 18 in. (45 cm) long. There is also a form, 'Variegata', with cream-variegated leaves, which is now almost unobtainable. Brownish purple flowers with fleshy petals, produced directly from the root at soil level, sometimes appear in early spring. Give average watering, wash the leaves occasionally and repot only every three to four years. Dry air will result in brown leaf tips; MWT 40°F (4°C). Increase by removing suckers in spring and potting separately.

Asplenium. The bird's nest fern, *A. nidus*,** inhabits rain forests in Asia and Australia and needs plenty of moisture and warmth. The glossy light green leaves each form a single blade in a rosette with a central funnel and can grow very large, up to 3 ft (90 cm) long in the wild. A warm bathroom is ideal, as it likes shade and humidity; MWT 60°F (16°C). It can be bound on to peat on a 'raft' (made with short lengths of wood crossing at right angles) or hung from the ceiling in a hanging basket.

Azalea. See *Rhododendron*.

Begonia. This genus is a large and varied one, and it would be quite possible to fill the house with an assortment of begonias, both flowering and foliage kinds, and nothing else.

The rex begonia** hybrids are perhaps the best known of the foliage sorts, with their large richly coloured leaves in purple, plum and magenta, marked with silver and green, or with a green background and yellow, grey and pink. They are bushy plants, slowly growing to about 1 ft (30 cm) and rather more wide (see p.30).

The Iron Cross begonia, *B. masoniana*, has a deep brown cross in the centre of the corrugated green leaves and reaches a similar size. Where space is limited, the eyelash begonia, *B. boweri*, with hairy margins to the leaves, and B. 'Tiger', with green leaves spotted brown, both make good decorative bushy plants, about 8 in. (20 cm) wide. All these begonias* have rhizomatous roots.

The cane or shrubby begonias* are tall plants to 3 or 4 ft (90–120 cm). The elephant's ear begonia, B. scharffii (B. haageana), has hairy leaves 10 in. (25 cm) long, with crimson undersides and rosy pink flowers in winter. B. metallica has shiny green leaves and large clusters of pink flowers borne for most of the year. This group has fibrous roots.

The many tuberous hybrids*, with double flowers in summer, have no equal the gorgeous colouring and shape of the blooms. Most are in single shades, although there are some very pretty fringed kinds with the margins of the petals outlined in a different colour.

The pendula begonias,* with single flowers, are excellent for trailing over the sides of hanging baskets or pots and are also tuberous-rooted. So too is the charming B. sutherlandii,* with slender reddish stems in quantity arching to form a mound, pointed leaves and a profusion of orange flowers all summer and autumn.

The Reiger begonias** again are superb flowering pot plants, whose large single or small double flowers in beautiful colours appear continuously in summer and winter. Height is about 9 in. (23 cm) with the same spread, but they are 'throwaway' plants and not worth keeping once they have finished flowering (see p.37).

The same applies to the numerous semperflorens hybrids or wax begonias,* with white, pink or red flowers and green or deep wine-red leaves. These flower from June to November and are then discarded. They can be kept going in winter, but usually the light is not sufficient to ensure good colouring or even flowering.

All begonias prefer shade rather than bright light, particularly the leafy ones. They need good humidity, but only moderate watering as too much easily rots the fibrous shoots or tubers. MWT 50°F (10°C) for the foliage and Reiger kinds. With tuberous-rooted sorts, keep the tubers frost-free and dry in winter, start growing in moist peat at a temperature of 60°F (16°C) in early spring, then pot into compost.

Propagate the rhizomatous begonias by division, the remainder by stem cuttings. Rex begonias can also be increased from leaf cuttings. An entire leaf is removed, cut across the main veins and laid flat on compost, weighted down. It should be kept warm and humid until new plants have formed from the veins. Watch for mildew.

Beloperone. The shrimp plant, B. guttata,* is one of the easiest houseplants and will flower all year if allowed to. The 2-in. (5 cm) long flower heads consist of overlapping salmon-pink bracts, with tubular, purple-spotted, white flowers protruding from them, on a bushy evergreen plant. In its native Mexico it grows 3 feet (90 cm) tall. Feed in summer, but stop in autumn and keep on the dry side, MWT 50°F (10°C), to allow to rest. Cut it back in early spring by half and repot. Increase from tip cuttings. Watch for red spider mite (see p.40).

Billbergia. See under Aechmea.

Browallia. B. speciosa* is a pretty plant which is almost smothered in blue, white or lavender, open, trumpet-shaped flowers, continuing for many weeks in spring and summer, or summer and autumn, depending on when the seed is sown. Height is nearly 1 ft (30 cm), with arching stems, and it is a good plant for hanging baskets. Ample light with some sun is required, enough water to keep the soil moist, but not sodden, and cool conditions, around 60°F (16°C). It is an annual, easily grown from seed sown in spring.

Calathea. See under Maranta.

Campanula. The Italian bellflower, C. isophylla,* is a native of northern Italy and almost hardy. It produces a profusion of light blue, open, bell flowers 1 in. (2.5 cm) wide, on trailing stems 9 in. (23 cm) long, from July to November. There is also a white form, 'Alba'. It does best in a light, even sunny place, particularly in a hanging basket, and needs daily watering while in flower, as well as deadheading. As it ceases flowering, new shoots appear and the old stems should be removed. The plant is then rested over winter in cool conditions, no more than 46°F (8°C), and repotted in peat-based compost. Increase by division or tip cuttings (see p.40).

Left: *Beloperone guttata* will grow leggy unless cut back (see p.39)

Right: *Campanula isophylla* has deservedly become a more common houseplant in Britain (see p.39)

Capsicum.**   The ornamental capsicums, relatives of the peppers which are the source of cayenne and paprika, have been selected for their appearance rather than their flavour. The fruits are in fact edible, but very hot. They appear in late autumn to mid-winter and are conical, upward-pointing and coloured yellow, red and purple on the same plant, which is bushy and on average 10 in. (25 cm) high and wide. Regarded as disposable plants, they need plenty of water and overhead spraying while fruiting, with sun at some time during the day (see p.12).

Ceropegia.   Hearts entangled, *C. woodii,** is an intriguing plant with waterfalls of stems festooned with thick heart-shaped leaves, of dark green covered in white marbling. Given sun or very good light, it will produce tubular flowers in the leaf-joints, of light purple with dark tips, throughout the summer and autumn. Water moderately, keep on the dry side in winter, MWT 45°F (7°C), and repot every second or third year. Cut straggly stems back by half to make them develop sideshoots. It is easily rooted from cuttings.

Chamaedorea.   The parlour palm, *C. elegans,*** and other palms, such as *Howeia forsterana* and the pigmy date palm, *Phoenix roebelenii*, can be excellent houseplants. They grow slowly, prefer slight shade, have a graceful habit and require only moderate watering; MWT 50°F (10°C). However, they are prone to infection by scale insect which, because of their many leaflets, is difficult to eradicate. Good humidity will help to prevent this. When young, repot the plants every spring, and after four years or so, repot every two or three years and feed regularly. Brown-tipped leaves may mean too dry an atmosphere or too much lime in the compost.

Chlorophytum.   The spider plant, *C. comosum* 'Variegatum',* is aptly named for its long drooping stems ending in plantlets. It is a handsome and easily grown plant, with a rosette of narrow arching leaves, each 1 ft (30 cm) long, striped yellow or white down the centre. Good light ensures good leaf variegation; MWT 40°F (4°C). Small white flowers may also be produced in the summer, separately or with the plantlets. It grows rapidly and needs frequent repotting and watering, which will also prevent the leaf tips turning brown. Increase by cutting off and potting the plantlets (see p.62).

Left: *Codiaeum variegatum pictum*, known as croton and also, appropriately, as Joseph's coat (see p.42)

Right: *Cryptanthus bivittatus*, a bromeliad which is easy to grow (see p.42)

Chrysanthemum.* Pot chrysanthemums are now sold as flowering plants all the year round. They have been treated chemically to restrict the height to about 1 ft (30 cm) and pinched out to produce many sprays of flowers, which last for some two months. While in bloom, they should be watered well and given good light and a temperature of 50–60°F (10–16°C). After that, they can either be discarded or, having removed the dead flowers, they can be repotted into larger containers and fresh compost, when they will return to their natural height of 2 to 3 ft (60–90 cm). They can also be planted outdoors, but will not survive the winter.

Cineraria. See *Senecio*.

Cissus. The kangaroo vine, *C. antarctica*,* is native to Australia. It attaches itself to a support by tendrils and has evergreen leaves which are toothed, glossy and shaped like beech leaves, only a little larger. It grows about 6 to 12 in. (15–30 cm) a year and makes an attractive well-clothed climber. Preferring cool conditions and a little shade, it is ideal for north-facing windows, halls, landings and corners of unheated rooms; MWT 40°F (4°C). Moderate watering and a humid atmosphere prevent the leaves discolouring and withering.

The grape ivy, *C. rhombifolia*,* often confused with *Rhoicissus rhomboidea*, comes from Natal in South Africa. It climbs rapidly by means of tendrils to 12 ft (3.6 m), but if pinched back will become somewhat bushy, and has glossy, diamond-shaped, toothed leaves. The cultivar 'Ellen Danica' is more graceful and less tall, with deeply cut and toothed lobed leaves. They do best in a little shade, too much light making the leaves yellowish green, with plenty of water, average humidity and some form of support; MWT 45°F (7°C).

Increase both by tip cuttings rooted in a temperature of 70°F (21°C).

× Citrofortunella. The calamondin, × *C. mitis*,** is a charming miniature orange tree, with diminutive fruits about 1 in. (2.5 cm) in diameter to match. These are edible but bitter and make good marmalade. An evergreen plant, it grows 12 to 18 in. (30–45 cm) tall and has fragrant white flowers in spring. The oranges begin to ripen in late summer. It needs a sunny place and can go outside in summer. It also requires humidity from overhead spraying, which will help the flowers set fruit. Water moderately and feed while growing, then keep dryish in winter, MWT 50°F

(10°C). Increase by tip cuttings rooted in a temperature of 75° (24°C). Watch for scale.

Codiaeum. The croton, *C. variegatum pictum*,** is not a new houseplant by any means and, after its introduction from Polynesia in 1863, numerous hybrids were developed which adorned many Victorian homes. They are highly decorative, with evergreen leaves in yellow, pink, green, orange, red, white and brown, often having four colours on one leaf in blotches and stripes. But they are temperamental. They need steady high temperatures, preferably about 70°F (21°C), no draughts, a very moist atmosphere and frequent watering, together with good light and weekly feeding; MWT 60°F (16°C). Watch for scale insect and red spider mite; leaf drop indicates lack of water, dry air or draughts and pale leaves mean too little light (see p.41).

Coleus. The flame nettle, *C. blumei*,* usually grown in the form of its hybrids, is valued for its brilliant gaily coloured leaves, which far outdo the many insignificant flowers in their effect. Unfortunately, in Britain they are short-term plants for the summer and autumn and in the poor light of winter their leaves fade to an anonymous beige. The leaves may be heavily fringed and toothed, even jagged, at the edges, and ruffled, while the colour combinations are dazzling. Average height is about 2 ft (60 cm), but in optimum conditions – overhead light, plenty of warmth and water and good compost – they will grow to 4 ft (1.2 m) tall and 2 ft (60 cm) wide. Pinch out the tips of shoots to keep them short and bushy, and remove flower spikes. Increase from seed sown in spring in 60–70°F (16–21°C) (see p.2).

Cordyline. This genus of shrubs and trees from Australasia and eastern Asia is notable for the colourful foliage, in a range of pink, red, magenta, purple and cream flushed pink, on a green background. As houseplants, the leaves are 6 to 12 in. (15–30 cm) long, on a central stem 2 to 3 ft (60–90 cm) high. Plenty of water, good humidity and ample light provide healthy plants; MWT 55°F (13°C). Leaf drop is due to dry air or too little water, poor colour to lack of light. Increase by offsets.

Cryptanthus. The earth stars or starfish bromeliads, species of *Cryptanthus*, are dwarf bromeliads. Their evergreen leaves are coloured and marked in green, silver, brown, magenta, grey, rose-pink and white, depending on the species or variety, and are 6 to 12 in. (15–30 cm) long, mostly in the form of flattened rosettes. A peat-based compost and good light and humidity are all they need; MWT 50°F (10°C). Water and feed as for bromeliads generally. Increase by plantlets (see p.41).

Ctenanthe. See under *Maranta*.

Cyclamen.* These are very popular flowering plants, especially at Christmas time, with the reflexed petals of their pink, white, red, crimson or magenta flowers and, even when these have faded, the decorative white-marbled leaves. The new 'mini' cyclamen, only about 5 in. (12.5 cm) high and sometimes fragrant, are a delightful addition to the enormous range available. Cool temperatures of around 55–60°F (13–16°C) while growing and flowering, careful watering and frequent overhead misting are essential to success and will prevent wilting and red spider mite infestation. Yellowing leaves indicate too much water or draughts. Water from the top or bottom, but do not splash the leaves or stems and make sure the compost drains well. After flowering, feed and water until the leaves die down naturally and keep quite dry in a warm place until July. Then, as new growth starts, repot in fresh acid compost, half burying the corm, water moderately at first and shade for some of the day. The plant can be put outdoors until September. Once it is growing well, begin liquid feeding until the buds show, then stop until after flowering (see p.16).

Cyperus. The name umbrella plant is applied to *C. alternifolius*,* the more common species, growing to 4 ft (1.2 m), and to *C. diffusus*, 1 to 2 ft (30–60 cm) high. The stems carry a crown of narrow leaves, fanning out like the spokes of an umbrella, particularly effective in *C. alternifolius* 'Variegatus', with white-striped leaves. They are thirsty plants, best grown in pots placed in saucers of water,

Cyperus alternifolius, from Madagascar, inhabits bogs in the wild

which are constantly topped up and never allowed to dry out. Otherwise, they are not choosy and thrive in shade or good light and some humidity; MWT 50°F (10°C). Increase by division in spring.

Dieffenbachia.*** Commonly known as dumb cane, because the leaves are said to cause blisters on the tongue if eaten, these are handsome foliage plants, but very poisonous. They have fleshy stems to 5 ft (1.5 m) high in favourable environments and large 9-in. (23 cm) long leaves, heavily spotted and marked with cream or white. Forms of *D. maculata* (*D. picta*) are the chief ones grown, such as 'Exotica' and 'Marianne', the latter with only the edge of the leaf green. Humidity and plenty of light, but not summer sun, keep the leaves in good condition. Draughts or low winter temperatures will result in leaf drop and dry air in brown leaf edges. If the leaves fall, cut the main stem back to a few inches and it will sprout sideshoots. Water normally in summer, moderately in winter, MWT 60°F (16°C). Increase by suckers, or use the top few inches of stem as a cutting and root in plenty of warmth, 75–80°F (24–27°C).

Dizygotheca. The false aralia, *D. elegantissima*,*** hails from Australasia and is an elegant upright plant with narrow, dark olive-green leaflets much serrated at the edges, carried in clusters of seven to ten. It is slow-growing to about 5 ft (1.5 m) in twelve years, but can be temperamental, readily shedding its leaves as a result of draughts, dry air, cold or fluctuating temperatures. Plenty of humidity, an even warm temperature of 60°F (16°C) or more, and compost at a similar temperature are vital. Keep in good light, repot at two to three-year intervals when mature and feed occasionally. Watch for red spider mite and scale insect.

Dracaena.*** Yet another genus of fine foliage houseplants, the dracaenas show considerable variation from one to the other. *D. sanderiana* is an upright plant with narrow grey-green leaves edged in white sheathing the stem; it produces sideshoots. *D. surculosa* (*D. godseffiana*) is a low-growing shrubby species, whose dark green oval leaves are spotted lavishly with cream. *D. marginata* 'Tricolor' has a trunk 4 to 5 ft (1.2–1.5 m) tall, with a rosette at the top of arching, very narrow leaves 15 in. (38 cm) long, striped in green, cream and rose-pink. *D. fragrans* 'Massangeana' has a large rosette of glossy, broad, arching leaves sprouting from ground level, each striped widely down the centre with yellow. Treat as for codiaeums.

Epiphyllum.** These cacti are epiphytic or tree-dwelling, like the bromeliads, and perch on rotting vegetation in the forks of trees. The hybrids grown today, known as orchid or water lily cacti, have exquisitely beautiful flowers in white, pink, yellow, red or salmon, appearing in May to June and sometimes again in autumn. Height is 1 to 2 ft (30–60 cm) and they need supporting with stakes and ties. Water well when the whole compost is nearly dry, keep in good light with sun in winter, supply average humidity and repot every two to three years. In winter they should be allowed to rest in cool dry conditions, MWT 40°F (4°C), without drying out completely. Cut one or two of the oldest stems down to the base if flowering poorly. Increase by tip cuttings in summer or by seed.

Epipremnum. The devil's ivy, *E. aureum* (*Scindapsus aureus*),** from the Solomon Islands, is a fleshy-stemmed twining plant with strikingly variegated leaves, much splashed and spotted with yellow. The cultivar 'Marble Queen' is so heavily variegated as to be virtually a white-leaved plant and 'Golden Queen' is a similar form but in deep yellow. Both grow more slowly than the species. Small aerial roots are produced from the stems and, if trained into a moss stick, this will lead to larger leaves. Water well while growing and supply plenty of humidity. The species prefers a little shade, but not too much otherwise it becomes plain green, while the cultivars should have good light to retain their variegation; MWT 50°F (10°C). Use a peat-based compost and increase by potting up side stems from the base which have already rooted (see p.19).

Episcia.*** The flame violets, as they are called, are small ground-covering plants with oval, often quilted leaves, picked out in light green along the veins, and red or orange-red flowers. Their requirements are similar to *Fittonia* (see p.47).

Euphorbia. The poinsettia, *E. pulcherrima*,** is very popular at Christmas time with its striking red 'petals'. These are in fact bracts, crowning the top of each shoot to form a bushy plant up to 2 ft (60 cm) tall. New varieties have white, pink or crimson bracts on short plants 9 to 12 in. (23–30 cm) high. Flowers can last until May, during which time the poinsettia needs plenty of water, an even temperature of at least 60°F (16°C) and copious misting, together with good light. Afterwards, it can either be discarded, or the stems may be cut down to a few inches and the plant repotted. New shoots will appear and, to encourage the development of red or coloured bracts, keep the plant in complete darkness for fourteen hours each night during October and November, then allow it natural daylengths (see p.22).

Exacum. The Persian violet, *E. affine*,* is a 'throwaway' flowering plant, but so neat, floriferous and easy to look after that it is well worth having in the house for the summer. It lives up to its namesake too, as it is heavily fragrant. About 6 in. (15 cm) high, it is covered in light purple, gold-centred flowers from June to October. Good light and frequent misting, together with normal watering, will keep it growing well and faded flowers should be removed to ensure continuous blooming. It is easily raised from seed sown in late summer or early spring in a temperature of 65°F (16°C).

× **Fatshedera.** An elegant tall shrub, × *F. lizei** is grown for its evergreen leaves, which resemble very large, well-lobed, ivy leaves and betray its hybrid parentage (it is a cross between *Fatsia* and *Hedera* or ivy). There is also a variegated form with cream tips to the leaves, which is more decorative but less easy to grow. It is partially climbing and requires staking or other support, reaching 6 ft (1.8 m) or more. Almost hardy, it prefers cool temperatures and a little shade, but more light for the variegated form, with average watering and humidity. Increase from cuttings in midsummer.

Fatsia. One of the parents of the above, *F. japonica*** has large, lobed, evergreen leaves and is a tall bushy plant. It has the same cultivation needs.

Ficus. The popular rubber plant, *F. elastica* 'Decora',* makes a handsome upright plant with its large, glossy, oval leaves and grows easily and rapidly, reaching the ceiling of many homes. Other members of the genus are equally attractive. *F. deltoidea* (*F. diversifolia*)* is a small, slow-growing, bushy species, with rounded triangular leaves and small yellow fruits like marbles. It is sometimes known as the mistletoe fig. *F. pumila* (*F. repens*),** the creeping fig, has trailing stems clothed in small dark green leaves and can be allowed to trail or be trained as a climber. *F. benjamina,** the weeping fig, grows into a graceful small tree up to 6 ft (2 m) high, with arching shoots and pointed glossy leaves.

For the last three species good humidity is important, otherwise the leaves fall. The rubber plant needs regular leaf-cleaning and all like temperatures above 50°F (10°C). Water moderately in summer, but less in winter. A little shade suits the small species, while some sun is advisable for the tree-like kinds. Repot every other year and increase by cuttings. Watch for scale insect and red spider mite.

Fittonia. The mosaic plant, *F. verschaffeltii argyroneura,**** is a native of Peruvian rain forests and has creeping stems, with delicate white netting on dark green leaves. The miniature form, 'Snakeskin', is easier to grow and particularly suitable for bottle gardens. High humidity, some shade and a good deal of water in summer are necessary for fittonias. In winter water sparingly, MWT 55°F (13°C), although for 'Snakeskin' 45°F (7°C) is satisfactory. Keep away from draughts. Increase from cuttings of the rooted trailing stems (see p.63).

Fuchsia.* Among the most delightful of flowering plants, fuchsias take kindly to container cultivation and indoor growing. Coolish conditions in summer, in slight shade or good light but not full sun, frost-free in winter and moderate watering are all they ask. There are many beautiful hybrids, single and double flowered, bushy and trailing. (For further details, see the Wisley handbook on fuchsias.)

Gloxinia. See *Sinningia*.

Grevillea. The Australian silk oak, *G. robusta,** is an evergreen tree 165 ft (50 m) tall in its native land. In the home it is a graceful upright plant, growing quite quickly to 10 ft (3 m) high if well suited, with feathery frond-like leaves. It requires average watering, feeding and humidity, and good light but shade from bright sun in summer. Keep cool in winter, MWT 45°F (7°C), and repot each spring (see p.47).

Guzmania. See under *Aechmea*.

Hedera.* The ivies are universally popular for their attractive leaf shape and colouring and for their habit, which enables them to be grown as climbers or trailers. The small-leaved forms of the common ivy, *H. helix*, vary enormously from plain green to variegated or speckled in cream, yellow or white, grey-green or flushed with pink, alone or in combination. Some good varieties are 'Goldheart' ('Jubilee'), with a golden centre; 'Luzii', speckled light green; 'Glacier', grey-green and cream; 'Eva', with white margins; 'Sagittifolia', with a long narrow central lobe; and 'Buttercup', with pale yellow young leaves. An attractive large-leaved ivy is *H. canariensis* 'Gloire de Marengo' ('Variegata'), which has irregular grey-green and cream mottling and red stems. Cool temperatures suit ivies best, some humidity, as hot dry air encourages red spider mite and withering leaves, good light for the variegated kinds and moderate watering. They are easily increased from stem cuttings pinned down flat on the compost surface.

45

Hibiscus. The hybrids of *H. rosa-sinensis*** make extremely pretty pot plants, bearing large funnel-shaped flowers of pink, red or orange in summer and autumn. The variety *cooperi*, with leaves variegated cream and pink to deep red, is attractive even when not in bloom. Height is about 2 ft (60 cm), though 6 ft (1.8 m) is possible, and width 18 in. (45 cm). Plenty of warmth, light and humidity are necessary all year, ample water in summer and feeding from early June until September. Prune hard after flowering or in early spring, cutting back shoots by half or more; MWT 55°F (13°C). Increase by tip cuttings rooted in a temperature of 75°F (24°C).

Hippeastrum.* The amaryllis, as it is commonly known, is correctly a *Hippeastrum* hybrid and should not be confused with *Amaryllis belladonna*, quite a different plant. It has trumpet-shaped flowers 6 in. (15 cm) wide at the mouth, carried singly or severally at the top of the stem, in white or shades of red and pink, and strap-shaped leaves emerging from the large bulb. Plants are potted from January to March or earlier in individual 6-in. (15 cm) diameter pots, burying only half the bulb in the compost and watering in well. Keep in a temperature of 70°F (21°C) and water sparingly until growth is obvious, then moderately. Give good light for flowering. Afterwards, remove the dead flowers and feed until the leaves die down, then dry off in temperatures no lower than 40°F (4°C) until time to repot again in January.

Howeia (*Howea*). See under *Chamaedorea* (and also p.48).

Hoya. An easily grown evergreen climber, which may be trained into various shapes, is the wax flower, *H. carnosa*.* It will bloom in the second year from a stem cutting, the stiff clusters of pink wax-like flowers, each with a drop of nectar, appearing in summer and smelling sweetly in the evening and at night. Moderate watering, less in winter, and good light, are required; MWT 50°F (10°C). Owing to its fast growth, it should be repotted while young or fed with a high potash fertilizer. Lack of food, hard water or too much water produce yellow leaves.

Hypoestes. The polka dot plant, *H. phyllostachya** (long wrongly identified as *H. sanguinolenta*), has been much improved by selection in recent years and the unusual pink spots and blotches covering much of the dark green leaves make it as colourful as a flowering plant. The stronger the light, the better the colours, provided the leaves are not scorched. Height is 6 to 12 in. (15–30 cm) and it likes plenty of water while growing; MWT 50°F (10°C). Keep it bushy by pinching out the tips of shoots and use these for cuttings. Scale insect can be a major problem.

Impatiens. The busy lizzie, *I. walleriana** and its progeny, can be very busy indeed, profusely flowering all year if allowed to. But it is one of those plants which should be made to rest by lowering the winter temperature and decreasing the amount of water and light. All flower colours except blue are available, together with cream-variegated or crimson-green leaves and, in the most recent New Guinea Hybrids, green, yellow, red and bronze colourings. Plenty of water and a very humid atmosphere prevent buds, flowers and leaves dropping and ward off red spider mite. A sunny position and temperature of 75°F (24°C) maximum, MWT 50°F (10°C), are further aids to health. Pinch out the tips for bushier, more floriferous plants and root these in compost or water for increase (see p.29).

Jasminum. The jasmine, *J. officinale*,* must be one of the most sweetly scented flowering plants, with white flowers appearing all summer. A rampant climber, it needs a large container and plenty of wall space, but is otherwise easy to grow, being almost completely hardy. Water and feed well in summer, supply good light and humidity and repot in the growing season. Prune in early spring to fit its space.

J. polyanthum* flowers in winter from December to March, in a temperature of 60°F (16°C) or more, and needs ample light and warmth in summer to ripen the new growth. Increase both by division or cuttings.

Kalanchoe. The succulent *K. blossfeldiana** has rosettes of rounded fleshy leaves at ground level, from which come slender flowering stems, topped with clusters of

46

Above: the South American *Episcia cupreata* (left) likes a very humid atmosphere (see p.44); the lovely *Hibiscus rosa-sinensis* (right) belongs to the same family as mallow and hollyhock

Below: *Grevillea robusta* (left is grown for the attractive fern-like foliage (see p.45); the hippeastrum (right) is now a popular Christmas present

Howeia forsterana comes from Lord Howe Island in the South Pacific (see p.40)

small tubular flowers in red, yellow, orange or white. Mostly seen at Christmas, it is in fact available in flower at any time. From 12 to 18 in. (30–45 cm) high, there are also dwarf versions, about 6 in. (15 cm) tall, while the new Swiss hybrids, with much larger flowers, are 6 to 12 in. (15–30 cm) in height. Let the compost become almost dry between waterings, give good light and average humidity; MWT 50°F (10°C). After flowering, remove the stems, keep the plant nearly dry for several weeks and slightly shaded, then repot and treat normally. Increase from seed (see p.50).

Maranta.*** The prayer plants, varieties of *M. leuconeura*, are beautiful but demanding small foliage plants, with colourfully marked and often velvety-looking leaves. *M. l. kerchoveana* has brown splodges on the grey-green leaves and *M. l. leuconeura* (*M. l. massangeana*) white veining on a dark olive-green background; *M. l. erythrophylla* (*M. tricolor*) has red veining. They need a lot of humidity, high steady temperatures of 60–70°F (15–21°C) and a little shade in summer, but good light in winter, MWT 50°F (10°C). Lack of humidity is the greatest drawback, causing leaf browning and withering very quickly. Acid compost and soft water at room temperature are important; do not allow them to dry out. Increase by division (see p.50).

Calatheas and ctenanthes are similar to marantas in general colouring, but up to twice the size, at 2 to 3 ft (60–90 cm) high, and more difficult, as they need even greater humidity.

Monstera. The Swiss cheese plant, *M. deliciosa* (*M. pertusa*),** is a striking and magnificent plant with large leaves, at least 15 in. (38 cm) long and nearly as wide, which are pierced and serrated. Naturally a climbing plant with aerial roots, it grows rapidly to 6 ft (1.8 m) and should be trained on to a moss stick, which is kept moist by spraying; if it gets too tall, cut the top off and root it as a cutting. Some shade, good humidity and a temperature of 65°F (18°C), with watering at sufficient intervals to allow the compost to dry out somewhat, will suit it; MWT 50°F (10°C). If holes and slashes do not develop on the new leaves, some aspect of its care is wrong. Moving the plant to a completely different position will often put matters right (see p.9).

Neoregelia. See under *Aechmea* (and p.25).

Nephrolepis. The ladder fern, *N. exaltata*,* is a fast-growing elegant fern from tropical regions, but will nevertheless stand comparatively low temperatures, down to 50°F (10°C). Its light green, arching fronds are deeply cut into feathery segments and a well-grown plant can be 6 ft (1.8 m) wide, though it will be less in the average pot or hanging basket. There are several attractive cultivars which grow less rapidly. Provide plenty of humidity and acid compost and feed frequently. Increase by runners, pegging these into compost and then potting the plantlets separately (see p.50).

Passiflora. The passion flower, *P. caerulea*,* is a vigorous climber with remarkable blue, white and purple flowers, which are shortlived but produced in quantity between July and September. The plant grows rapidly and attaches itself by tendrils. It requires as much light as possible, plenty of water while growing, average humidity and normal summer temperatures, MWT 40°F (4°C). In a conservatory it may produce edible but rather insipid fruit. In spring cut it back hard and repot. Propagate from seed or by cuttings (see p.26).

Pelargonium.* Pelargoniums are excellent good-tempered houseplants, mostly flowering freely and continuously all year if allowed to. Zonal pelargoniums – the plants most commonly called geraniums and often used for bedding – have a dark band on the upper surface of the leaves and clusters of small flowers. Regal pelargoniums have funnel-shaped frilly flowers, three or four in a loose cluster. Ivy-leaved geraniums are trailing, with fleshy pointed-lobed leaves, sometimes mottled white as in 'Crocodile', or variegated grey-green, white and pink, with white flowers, as in 'L'Elégante'. Scented-leaved geraniums have pungent finely dissected leaves, smelling of lemon, eucalyptus, apple, rose, or sandalwood. The miniatures grow to only about 8 in. (20 cm) and often have brightly coloured leaves as well as brilliant flowers.

Suitable for sunny windowsills, even at midday in summer, the pelargoniums do not need humidity, but require regular watering and drying out between applications. Cut the regals back in summer after flowering and repot them after a rest at this time. Pinch back stems of others to keep the plants bushy and cut back hard in early spring, as growth starts again with regular watering. In winter, keep frost-free and almost dry. Increase by tip cuttings in late summer, or the new F_1 hybrids from seed sown in heat in January or February. Watch for whitefly on regals and rust and red spider mite on all. (See also the Wisley handbook on pelargoniums.)

Peperomia. There are a number of different peperomias, mostly with attractive leaves, but the best known and least difficult to grow is *P. caperata*,** with corrugated, dark green, heart-shaped leaves about 2 in. (5 cm) long and unusual hooked spikes of white flowers on reddish stems. A small bushy plant to about 8 in. (20 cm) tall, it is neat and slow-growing. It needs plenty of humidity and without this will drop its leaves quickly. Water moderately in summer, less in winter and keep in good light; MWT 55°F (13°C). Increase by leaf cuttings, as for *Saintpaulia*.

Above: *Kalanchoe blossfeldiana* (left) does well on a sunny windowsill; one of the main requirements of marantas (right) and their relatives is high humidity (see pp.46 and 48)

Below: *Nephrolepis exaltata* can be propagated at any time of year from runners (see p.49)

Philodendron. The sweetheart vine, *P. scandens*,* owes its name to the pointed heart-shaped leaves, 6 to 12 in. (15–30 cm) long when full grown, with a glossy surface. It is a climber, twining round its support with fleshy stems, and amenable to shade; MWT 50°F (10°C). Grow as a trailer or train the aerial roots round a moist moss stick, and water well in summer, moderately in winter. High humidity is important. Increase by cuttings in a temperature of 75°F (24°C).

Phoenix. See under *Chamaedorea*.

Pilea. The aluminium plant, *P. cadieri*,* belongs to the same plant family as the stinging nettle. Its 3-inch (7.5 cm) long oval leaves are patched and banded with silver, giving them a metallic gleam and accounting for its common name. Height is about 12 in. (30 cm), though a newer form, 'Minima', is more compact and does not become straggly with age. *P. involucrata* is quite a different colour, with bronze-green corrugated leaves. Pileas need plenty of humidity to avoid leaf drop, moderate watering and good light; MWT 50°F (10°C). Pinch back the stems to keep them bushy. Increase by tip cuttings (see p.22).

Platycerium. The stag's horn fern, *P. bifurcatum*,* is an epiphyte, living in trees and rooting into vegetable debris which collects in the branches. From tropical regions, it needs plenty of humidity to maintain its softly hairy, forked, antler-like fronds in good condition. These are the fertile spore-bearing fronds, whereas the thin, rounded, plate-like, green 'leaves', which turn brown and papery, are sterile fronds and act eventually as an anchor, sheathing their support. It is happiest in a hanging basket or attached to tree bark; MWT 50°F (10°C). Grow in a peat-based compost and water moderately.

Primula.* The primulas – *P. obconica*, the fragrant *P. malacoides* or fairy primrose, and the smaller *P. sinensis* – are pretty flowering pot plants to cheer up the winter and easily grown. They last in flower from December to the end of March or even longer, provided faded blooms are removed, pink, blue, mauve, yellow, white and red being the usual colours. Keep them well watered, humid, in good light and cool, at 55–60°F (13–16°C); high temperatures or dry air will encourage red spider mite. *P. malacoides* is usually shortlived, but *P. sinensis* and *P. obconica* may be potted in fresh compost and put outside in a cool place with a little shade until autumn, then brought in and again kept in low temperatures (see p.52).

Pteris. The generic name of the ribbon fern, *P. cretica*,** comes from the Greek word *pteron*, meaning a feather. The feathery quality of the fronds is emphasized in the form 'Albo-Lineata', which has all its veins marked in white, making it doubly attractive. Growing 12 to 18 in. (30–45 cm) high, the plant should be given shade, plenty of humidity, acid compost and soft water; MWT 50°F (10°C).

Rhipsalidopsis. See under *Schlumbergera*.

Rhododendron.* The azaleas grown as winter-flowering pot plants are mainly derived from the Chinese *R. simsii*. Their glamorous frilled flowers may be pink, red, white, salmon, crimson and all shades of these, usually very double, and are carried on a small evergreen shrub. When flowering in mid-winter, they need watering daily, sometimes twice daily, and frequent overhead spraying, otherwise the leaves will drop and the plants become infested with red spider mite. A well ventilated but moist atmosphere and temperature of 55–60°C (13–16°C) are best, with ample light but not direct sun. Lower temperatures prolong flowering. Soft water and acid compost are essential. After flowering, cut back all shoots by one eighth of their length to encourage the growth of new shoots for flowering next winter, pot into a slightly larger pot, using ericaceous or acid compost, and put outdoors in a lightly shaded place when the risk of frost is past. Feed every two weeks from that time and remember to keep the plant watered. In September bring it in, stop feeding and water sparingly. The warmer indoor temperature will encourage flower buds to appear and watering should then be increased (see p.19).

Rhoicissus. See under *Cissus*.

Above: *Primula malacoides* is treated as an annual but is very free-flowering (see p.51)

Below: 'Tricolor', a diminutive form of *Saxifraga stolonifera*, appreciates bright light

Saintpaulia. The much loved African violet, S. *ionantha*,** is now so greatly hybridized that all shades of purple, blue, pink, crimson, white and magenta can be found, together with coloured-edged and double flowers. Miniature and trailing kinds are also available, as well as the normal compact rosette-forming plants. Given plenty of light, but shade from strong sun, they flower all year and most profusely in summer. A steady draught-free temperature of 60°F (16°C) and water given at the same temperature will suit them. Peat-based compost is preferable, kept moist but never sodden, and watering should be infrequent. Humidity is very important, although the hairy leaves should not be misted or sprayed as they can be damaged. Increase by leaf cuttings, by removing a leaf with the stalk attached; push it into damp compost to about half the length of the stalk and keep in a humid atmosphere. Plants can also be increased by division or seed (see p.6).

Sansevieria. Mother-in-law's tongue, S. *trifasciata*,* comes from tropical Africa and Asia. Its cultivar 'Laurentii', the one grown as a houseplant, has stiff, upright, fleshy leaves, narrowly edged with yellow, about 15 in. (38 cm) tall. With sufficient warmth and light, it will produce a fragrant white flower spike. Water moderately in summer, sparingly in winter, MWT 50°F (10°C). Too much water and too low a temperature in winter result in the stems rotting at soil level. Increase by division.

Saxifraga. Mother of thousands, S. *stolonifera*,* is so named for its ability to produce plantlets at the end of thread-like stems hanging from the central rosette of leaves. The leaf colouring is dark green veined with white, with an undersurface of crimson, and delicate, yellow-centred, white flowers are produced in airy clusters on 12-in. (30-cm) stems in May and June. The very attractive form 'Tricolor' has white-edged leaves, flushed pink, but needs a higher temperature and is less easy to grow. The species itself is nearly hardy and does best in a temperature of 50–60°F (10–16°C), with a little shade or good light and moderate watering and humidity. Increase by potting the plantlets individually.

Schefflera. The umbrella tree, S. *actinophylla*,* is grown for its evergreen leaves, which consist of about seven drooping leaflets radiating from the leaf stem, the whole leaf being about 9 in. (12 cm) wide. It is good-tempered and does not require a great deal of warmth, accepting a temperature of about 50°F (10°C) in winter, or lower for short periods if kept on the dry side. Water freely in summer, sparingly in winter and place in good light or a little shade. Height is about 6 ft (1.8 m) in the home, though in its native Australia it can grow to 130 ft (40 m), and pinching out the growing tip will encourage branching. Watch for red spider mite and scale insect. Increase by stem cuttings, which need a temperature of 75°F (24°C) in the compost.

Schlumbergera. The Christmas cactus, with the awkward botanical name of *Schlumbergera × buckleyi** (formerly *Zygocactus truncatus*), is a profusely flowering plant from November until January. The bright magenta-pink flowers look like fuchsia blooms with protruding stamens and are produced at the end of flattened stems, which are divided into segments and have scalloped margins. It is an epiphytic or tree-dwelling cactus and grows in the same conditions as the bromeliads. A peat-based compost is advisable to start with, repotting in a soil-based kind as it matures, for it becomes very large, 2 ft (60 cm) and more across. Water moderately while flowering, give good light and spray overhead occasionally in a centrally heated room. After flowering, water sparingly and lower the temperature to 45–50°F (7–10°C) to allow it to rest. Repot annually in spring when young, every third year when mature, and put outside in light shade until September, when it should be taken back indoors. New shoots appear in midsummer and buds in October, so long as it is given the short daylengths normal in autumn. By keeping the temperature down to about 55°F (13°C), it is possible to delay flowering until Christmas, but the duration of this treatment will depend on individual plants.

The Easter cactus, *Rhipsalidopsis gaertneri*,* needs the same cultivation con-

ditions, except that its resting period is September to December rather than February to April; it should also receive natural daylengths in the autumn. Winter temperature should be about 65°F (18°C) and the buds appear from February.

Increase these cacti by cuttings of two to three stem segments, allowed to dry a day or two, in late spring or summer. Watch for mealy bug and root aphis; prone to bud drop.

Scindapsus. See *Epipremnum*.

Sedum. *S. sieboldii** is a succulent, with toothed round blue-grey leaves in pairs along its hanging stems. The whole plant grows to about 10 in. (25 cm) wide and from September to November bears heads of tiny purple-pink flowers. There is also a form, 'Medio-Variegatum', which has an irregular creamy yellow stripe to each leaf and grows more slowly. Easily cultivated, this sedum will stand winter temperatures down to 35°F (2°C). or 45°F (7°C) for the cultivar, especially if kept on the dry side. In summer it needs sunlight or plenty of light and moderate watering. The leaves turn purple in late autumn and can last well into winter, but the plant then dies back completely. Repot in spring and divide for increase.

Senecio. The cinerarias are colourful hybrids grouped under the name *S. × hybridus,** mainly derived from *S. cruentus* (*Cineraria cruenta*). Available in winter as flowering pot plants, they are disposable, but their profusion of daisy flowers in bright blue, white, magenta, salmon, pink or wine make them well worth growing, especially as they remain in bloom for at least six weeks. Depending on the type, height can vary from 9 to 24 in. (23–60 cm). A cool temperature, about 50–60°F (10–16°C), is important as they wilt easily. Good light, but not sun, and some humidity are also needed, together with careful watering to keep the compost moist but not waterlogged. Watch for greenfly.

The string of beads, *S. rowleyanus,** is an interesting oddity. The common name describes it exactly, as the leaves have been converted to solid round balls about ¼ in. (6 mm) in diameter, spaced at intervals along the thread-like stems, which trail or form mats of vegetation. It has fragrant purple and white flowers in autumn. As a succulent, it should be watered moderately in summer, about once a month in winter, with plenty of light and average humidity; MWT 40°F (4°C).

Setcreasea. The purple heart, *S. pallida* 'Purple Heart' (*S. purpurea*),* from Mexico, is a stiffly trailing plant used for ground-cover in the tropics. Its fleshy jointed stems are sheathed in narrow pointed leaves, both having an overall colour of deep purple, and in late summer it produces tiny purple-pink flowers. It grows vigorously in high temperatures and bright light, but fades in poor light. Plenty of water in summer and a moderate amount in winter will keep it healthy; MWT 50°F (10°C). The stem tips can be pinched out to encourage sideshoots and used as cuttings, which root easily in summer.

Sinningia.** The gloxinias or *Sinningia* hybrids have some of the most beautiful flowers among pot plants. Large, velvety and trumpet-shaped, 3 in. (7.5 cm) wide, there are as many as twelve on one plant, lasting for about two months and set off by green leaves up to 10 in. (25 cm) long. Height is 9 in. (23 cm) and colours are red, purple, pink, white and blue-mauve, with the Tiger race having spotting on the throat. They need shade from strong sunlight, plenty of water while growing, average summer temperatures and some humidity. After flowering, dry off gradually in the autumn and keep the tubers at about 50°F (10°C), then in spring repot and do not water until the leaves appear. Depending on their flowering time, which starts between June and August, they are potted from March to May. They can be raised from seed, sown at intervals in warmth, to bloom through the year.

Solanum. The winter cherry, *S. capsicastrum,**** belongs to the same genus as the

Opposite: the glowing colours of cinerarias cheer up the home in winter and early spring

tomato and potato. The small round bright red fruits are the size of marbles, scattered all over a bushy little plant about 9 in. (23 cm) tall. It is a 'throwaway' plant, available in early winter. To make sure it does not drop its fruits and leaves as soon as you get it, give it plenty of humidity by spraying at least once a day and put it with other plants. Place in good light and water well; MWT 55°F (13°C))see p.26)

Streptocarpus. * This may sound like an illness, but it is the generic name for the Cape primrose. These beautiful flowering plants from South Africa have funnel-shaped flowers with smooth or frilly petals, $1\frac{1}{2}$–$2\frac{1}{2}$ in. (4–6 cm) wide, in clusters on stems averaging 9 in. (23 cm) tall. The blue 'Constant Nymph' is the one generally grown. The Concorde group is especially pretty in a range of blue, lilac, purple and white and the Royal race has larger flowers; some kinds have dark pencilling in the throats. They flower from June to November or longer. Good light but not sun, ample water while flowering, much less in winter, and some humidity are factors in successful growing; MWT 45°F (7°C). Plants grow quickly and need feeding during the growing season. Increase by division in spring and repot annually.

Syngonium. Like the philodendrons and monsteras, S. podophyllum, * is a member of the arum family and is commonly known as the goosefoot plant, from the shape of the young leaves. The fleshy climbing stems produce aerial roots, so a moss stick is an ideal support. Cultivars with variegated leaves include 'Emerald Gem', with yellow veining; 'Greengold', with a yellow centre; and 'Imperial White', with green margins. Lots of humidity is essential; MWT 60°F (16°C). Normal watering, provided the compost does not start to dry out, and a good light for the variegated kinds, a little shade for the plain-leaved ones, will result in healthy plants. Increase from stem cuttings.

Thunbergia. Black-eyed Susan, T. alata, * is an annual climber, with flat, orange, brown-black centred flowers 2 in. (5 cm) wide all summer on a plant some 6 ft (2 m) tall, though it can be kept shorter and bushier by pinching out the tips and restricting the pot size. There are yellow- and white-flowered forms as well. Keep well watered and in bright light with some sun and average humidity. Discard old plants in autumn and grow from seed sown in a temperature of 65–75°F (18–25°C).

Tolmiea. The piggyback plant, T. menziesii, * is so named from its habit, unique among houseplants, of producing plantlets on the upper surface of the leaves where these join the leaf-stalks. It forms a bushy plant about 6 in. (15 cm) tall, of pleasant light green, and is very tolerant, except of heat and dry air. There is also a variegated form. It is nearly hardy, so does best in cool temperatures, MWT 40°F (4°C), with plenty of water and average humidity and good light or a little shade. It is very easy to increase from plantlets.

Tradescantia. * The name wandering Jew covers several genera, but the trades-cantias are the best known, plants with trailing jointed stems to 3 ft (90 cm) and pointed oval leaves in pairs, striped white or light yellow. T. fluminensis is the common one, with 'Variegata' having leaves striped yellow and 'Tricolor' pink-flushed on white stripes. If stems get straggly, cut them back hard and repot the plant. T. albiflora 'Albovittata' is altogether larger, with thicker stems and larger, more obviously striped leaves. White flowers may be produced. Water well in summer, sparingly in winter, supply good light and feed while growing; MWT 45°F (7°C). Increase by tip cuttings in summer (see p.58).

Vriesea. See under Aechmea.

Yucca. Although it may seem an unlikely plant to grow indoors, Y. elephantipes* is widely available, either as a foliage pot plant with a short trunk and cluster of leaves at the top, or as a dormant plant called a ti tree or happy plant. The ti cane – a piece of dried woody stem or cane – is planted vertically, or horizontally half-covered, in moist peat-based compost. With a temperature of 65–70°F (18–21°C), it will sprout a cluster of leaves at some point on the cane. Then supply average

Above: gloxinias are descended from a Brazilian species, *Sinningia speciosa* (see p.55)

Below: *Syngonium podophyllum* 'Emerald Gem' does best in a well lit position

Tradescantia should be given good light to preserve the leaf colours
(see p.56)

temperatures in summer, and water well while growing, sparingly during winter,
MWT 40°F (4°C).

Zebrina Also called wandering Jew and sometimes confused with the trades-
cantias, *Z. pendula** is striped dark green and silvery green with a purple underside. 'Quadricolor' has white added to these, all flushed purple and with a purple
underside; 'Purpusii' is coloured in varying shades of purple. They are exceedingly
attractive trailers, though slow-growing to about 1 ft (30 cm). Give plenty of light
and water moderately, less in winter, MWT 50°F (10°C). Too much food makes
them a uniform green.